PESCATARIAN

COOKBOOK

70 Recipes for Preparing at Home Healthy Fish and Seafood Dishes.

Maki Blanc

The trademarks that are used are without any consent, and the publication of the trademark is without permission or backing by the trademark owner. All trademarks and brands within this book are for clarifying purposes only and are owned by the owners themselves, not affiliated with this document.

Contents

Introduction

People are bringing more variety into their eating routines, and many want to add fish into their eating plans as eating certain fish species can add protein and hold fat admission down. A Pescatarian diet is an eating regimen that bars meat and poultry yet incorporates plant food varieties, fishes, dairy and eggs. Pescatarians can eat any fish and devour food from plants, dairy and eggs sources.

Pescatarians are vegetarians who fill their essential protein source with the help of seafood in their diet. The Pescatarian diet improves your diet and lifestyle habits. However, you will be eating undeniably a larger number of vegetables than meat, and vegetables will, in general, have fewer calories and less fat. In this way, you will have an eating routine normally lower in calories and fat admission.

This book promotes healthy eating and contains 70 different recipes that you can easily follow with the detailed ingredient list and easy-to-understand instructions list below each recipe. The recipe list contains breakfast, lunch, dinner, and snack recipes.

Chapter 1: The World of Pescatarian Breakfast Recipes

The basic thing more regrettable than a terrible breakfast is having nothing at all to eat in the morning. Fortunately, that will not be an issue for you. We have assembled a setup of the absolute best pescatarian breakfast recipes you would love to make yourself. Following are the recipes listed below:

1.1 Salmon Muffins Recipe

Preparation Time: 20 minutes

Cooking Time: 20 minutes

Serving: 4

Ingredients:

- Dried thyme, half teaspoon
- Smoked salmon, one and a half cup
- Large eggs, ten
- Garlic powder, half teaspoon
- Grated cheddar cheese, one cup
- Mozzarella cheese, one cup
- Chopped fresh dill, one cup
- Salt, to taste
- Black pepper, to taste

- Onion powder, one teaspoon
- Chopped cilantro, a quarter cup

Instructions:

1. Take a large bowl.
2. Add the eggs into the bowl.
3. Add the chopped dill into the bowl of eggs.
4. Add the garlic powder and onion powder into the bowl.
5. Add the cheddar and mozzarella cheese into the eggs.
6. Mix the eggs until all the mixture is uniformly mixed.
7. Add the dried thyme, smoked salmon meat, salt and pepper.
8. Add the egg mixture into the muffin tray.
9. Bake the muffins for about ten to fifteen minutes.
10. Add the chopped cilantro on top.
11. Your dish is ready to be served.

1.2 Shrimp and Scallion Pancakes Recipe

Preparation Time: 30 minutes

Cooking Time: 15 minutes

Serving: 4

Ingredients:

- Ground garlic, half teaspoon
- Salt, as required
- Shrimp, one cup
- Ground pepper, as required
- Scallions, one cup
- Cilantro as required
- Coconut oil, two tablespoon
- Tapioca flour, half cup
- Almond flour, half cup
- Coconut milk, one cup
- Ground ginger, half teaspoon

Instructions:

1. Mix in both the flours in a bowl.
2. Add the chopped or sliced scallions.
3. Add in the spices, deboned shrimps and cilantro.

4. Mix the ingredients carefully.

5. Add the mixture in small quantities in a pan.

6. Let the pancakes turn golden on both sides.

7. Add a little cilantro on top of the pancakes.

8. You can garnish the pancakes with any other thing that you prefer.

9. Your dish is ready to be served.

1.3 Avocado and Crab Toast Recipe

Preparation Time: 30 minutes

Cooking Time: 15 minutes

Serving: 4

Ingredients:

- Olive oil, two tablespoon

- Garlic powder, one tablespoon

- Salt to taste

- Pepper to taste

- Paprika, one tablespoon

- Onion diced, one cup

- Parsley, one tablespoon

- Crab meat, one cup

- Tomatoes, one cup

- Cheese slices, as required

- Bread slices, as required
- Avocado slices, one cup
- Yeast, two teaspoon

Instructions:

1. Take a pan and add the olive oil into it.
2. Heat the oil well.
3. Add parsley, garlic powder, paprika and tomatoes.
4. Cook them for five minutes.
5. Then you can add onions.
6. Cook the mixture again and keep stirring.
7. Add pieces of crab meat.
8. Continue to cook the ingredients for few minutes.
9. Lay the mixture onto a slice of bread.
10. Add the avocado slices on top of the meat.
11. Add a cheese slice on top and cover it with another bread slice.
12. Cook the bread slices on both sides.
13. You can serve it with any dip of your choice.
14. Your dish is ready to serve.

1.4 Smoked Salmon Toast Recipe

Preparation Time: 30 minutes

Cooking Time: 15 minutes

Serving: 4

Ingredients:

- Olive oil, two tablespoon
- Garlic powder, one tablespoon
- Salt to taste
- Pepper to taste
- Paprika, one tablespoon
- Onion diced, one cup
- Parsley, one tablespoon
- Smoked salmon, one cup
- Tomatoes, one cup
- Cheese slices, as required
- Bread slices, as required
- Yeast, two teaspoon

Instructions:

1. Take a pan and add the olive oil into it.
2. Heat the oil well.
3. Add parsley, garlic powder, paprika and tomatoes.

4. Cook them for five minutes.

5. Then you can add onions.

6. Cook the mixture again and keep stirring.

7. Add pieces of smoked salmon.

8. Continue to cook the ingredients for few minutes.

9. Lay the mixture onto a slice of bread.

10. Add a cheese slice on top and cover it with another bread slice.

11. Cook the bread slices on both sides.

12. You can serve it with any dip of your choice.

13. Your dish is ready to serve.

1.5 Shrimp and Guacamole Quesadillas Recipe

Preparation Time: 10 minutes

Cooking Time: 20 minutes

Serving: 2

Ingredients:

- Olive oil, two cups
- Garlic powder, one tablespoon
- Salt to taste
- Pepper to taste
- Paprika, one tablespoon
- Onion diced, one cup

- Parsley, one tablespoon
- Shrimp meat, one cup
- Tomatoes, one cup
- Guacamole paste, one cup
- Cheese slices, as required
- Tortilla sheets, four

Instructions:

1. Take a pan and add olive oil into it.
2. Heat the oil well.
3. Add parsley, garlic powder, paprika and tomatoes.
4. Cook them for five minutes.
5. Then you can add onions.
6. Cook the mixture again and keep stirring.
7. Add pieces of deboned shrimps.
8. Continue to cook the ingredients for few minutes.
9. Lay the mixture onto a tortilla sheet.
10. Add the guacamole mixture on top of the meat.
11. Add a cheese slice on top and cover it with another tortilla.
12. Cook the tortilla sheets on both sides.
13. You can serve it with any sauce of your choice.
14. Your dish is ready to be served.

1.6 Avocado and Tuna Salad Recipe

Preparation Time: 10 minutes

Cooking Time: 30 minutes

Serving: 2

Ingredients:

- Tuna pieces, half pound
- Maple syrup, one teaspoon
- Ground ginger, a quarter teaspoon
- Avocados, two
- Pecan pieces, two tablespoon
- Pepper, as required
- Cilantro, half cup
- Salt, a quarter teaspoon
- Greek yoghurt, as required
- Greek salad dressing, half cup

Instructions:

1. Peel the avocados and then cut them into large pieces.

2. Boil the tuna pieces, drain them and slice them into a bowl.

3. Mix all the ingredients along with the avocados and tuna.

4. In a bowl, add the salad dressing and beat it well.

5. Drizzle the dressing on top of the avocados and tuna mixture.

6. Your dish is ready to be served.

1.7 Salmon Burgers Recipe

Preparation Time: 20 minutes

Cooking Time: 20 minutes

Serving: 4

Ingredients:

- Burger buns, as required
- Minced salmon meat, one cup
- Bread crumbs, one cup
- Egg, one
- Chopped parsley, half cup
- Fresh chopped cilantro, half cup
- Salt, to taste
- Black pepper, to taste
- Olive oil, for frying
- Greek yoghurt, half cup
- Lemon juice, a quarter cup
- Fresh chopped dill, two tablespoon
- Butter, one tablespoon

Instructions:

1. Take a large bowl.

2. Add the salmon meat, salt, pepper, bread crumbs and egg into it.

3. Mix all the ingredients well.

4. Add the chopped cilantro and parsley into the mixture.

5. Mix the ingredients until they become smooth.

6. Shape the mixture into patties.

7. In a large pan, add the olive oil and cook the patties.

8. Cook the patties until they turn golden brown from both sides.

9. Meanwhile, in a small bowl, add the Greek yoghurt, lemon juice, and fresh dill.

10. Mix it to form a paste.

11. Add butter to your buns and heat them.

12. Add the salmon patty to the bread slice.

13. Add the paste on top of the patty and cover it with the burger bun.

14. The salmon burger is ready to be served.

1.8 Greek Salmon Burritos Recipe

Preparation Time: 10 minutes

Cooking Time: 20 minutes

Serving: 2

Ingredients:

- Olive oil, two cups
- Garlic powder, one tablespoon
- Salt to taste
- Pepper to taste
- Paprika, one tablespoon
- Onion diced, one cup
- Parsley, one tablespoon
- Salmon meat, one cup
- Tomatoes, one cup
- Jalapeno slices, as required
- Greek yoghurt, one cup
- Avocado slices, as required
- Tortilla sheets, four

Instructions:

1. Add the olive oil into a pan.
2. Heat the oil well.

3. Add the onions.

4. Cook the onions well until they turn soft.

5. Add parsley, garlic powder, paprika and tomatoes.

6. Cook them for five minutes.

7. Cook the mixture again and keep stirring.

8. Add pieces of salmon meat.

9. Continue to cook the ingredients for few minutes.

10.   Lay the mixture onto a tortilla sheet.

11.   Add the Greek yoghurt on top of the meat.

12.   Add the rest of the ingredients on top and roll it into a burrito.

13.   Heat the burrito.

14.   You can serve it with any sauce of your choice.

15.   Your dish is ready to be served.

1.9 Tomato, Asparagus and Tuna Muffins Recipe

Preparation Time: 20 minutes

Cooking Time: 20 minutes

Serving: 4

Ingredients:

- Chopped tomatoes, one cup
- Chopped asparagus, one cup
- Dried thyme, half teaspoon
- Tuna meat, one and a half cup
- Large eggs, ten
- Garlic powder, half teaspoon
- Grated cheddar cheese, one cup
- Mozzarella cheese, one cup
- Chopped fresh dill, one cup
- Salt, to taste
- Black pepper, to taste
- Onion powder, one teaspoon
- Chopped cilantro, a quarter cup

Instructions:

1. Take a large bowl.

2. Beat the eggs into the bowl.

3. Add the chopped dill into the bowl of eggs.

4. Add the garlic powder and onion powder into the bowl.

5. Add the cheddar and mozzarella cheese into the eggs.

6. Mix the eggs until all the mixture is uniformly mixed.

7. Add the dried thyme, chopped tomatoes, chopped asparagus and tuna meat, salt and pepper.

8. Add the egg mixture into the muffin tray.

9. Bake the muffins for about ten to fifteen minutes.

10. Add the chopped cilantro on top.

11. Your dish is ready to be served.

1.10 Salmon Scrambled Eggs Recipe

Preparation Time: 25 minutes

Cooking Time: 15 minutes

Serving: 4

Ingredients:

- Chopped garlic, two teaspoon
- Green onions, three tablespoon
- Tomato, half cup
- Salmon, two cups

- Chopped fresh dill, two tablespoon
- Vegetable oil, two tablespoon
- Soy sauce, two tablespoon
- Salt to taste
- Black pepper to taste
- Chopped fresh cilantro, one tablespoon
- Eggs, eight
- Chopped onions, two tablespoon

Instructions:

1. Heat a pan.
2. Add the oil into the pan.
3. Add the garlic and onions.
4. Add the salmon and cook on medium-high warmth for several seconds or until they begin to take on a changed tone.
5. Add in the tomato cook until delicate, however, to some degree crispy.
6. Turn down the warmth and pour the beaten eggs and leave to set for a couple of moments.
7. Scramble egg mixture.
8. Add in the soy sauce and chopped dill.
9. Add some salt and pepper.
10. Garnish it with chopped cilantro leaves.
11. Your dish is ready to be served.

1.11 Boiled Eggs and Sardine Salad Recipe

Preparation Time: 10 minutes

Cooking Time: 30 minutes

Serving: 2

Ingredients:

- Sardine pieces, half pound
- Lemon juice, one teaspoon
- Ground ginger, a quarter teaspoon
- Avocados, two
- Chopped almonds, two tablespoon
- Pepper, as required
- Cilantro, half cup
- Eggs, two
- Salt, a quarter teaspoon
- Greek yoghurt, as required
- Salad dressing, half cup

Instructions:

1. Boil the eggs, peel them, and then cut them into large pieces.
2. Boil the sardine pieces, drain them, and slice them into a bowl.

3. Mix all the ingredients along with the sardines and eggs.

4. In a bowl, add the salad dressing and beat it well.

5. Drizzle the dressing on top of the sardine and egg mixture.

6. The salad is ready to be served.

1.12 Tuna and Avocado Burgers Recipe

Preparation Time: 20 minutes
Cooking Time: 20 minutes
Serving: 4

Ingredients:

- Burger buns, as required
- Minced tuna meat, one cup
- Bread crumbs, one cup
- Avocado slices, as required
- Egg, one
- Chopped parsley, half cup
- Fresh chopped cilantro, half cup
- Salt, to taste
- Black pepper, to taste
- Olive oil, for frying
- Greek yoghurt, half cup
- Lemon juice, a quarter cup
- Fresh chopped dill, two tablespoon
- Butter, one tablespoon

Instructions:

1. Take a large bowl.

2. Add the tuna meat, salt, pepper, bread crumbs, and egg into it.

3. Mix all the ingredients well.

4. Add the chopped cilantro and parsley into the mixture.

5. Mix the ingredients until they become smooth.

6. Shape the mixture into patties.

7. In a large pan, add the olive oil and cook the patties.

8. Cook the patties until they turn golden brown from both sides.

9. Meanwhile, in a small bowl, add the Greek yoghurt, lemon juice and fresh dill.

10. Mix it to form a paste.

11. Add butter to your buns and heat them.

12. Add the tuna patty to the bread slice.

13. Add the paste on top of the patty.

14. Add the avocado slices on top of the paste and cover it with the burger bun.

15. The tuna and the avocado burger are ready to be served.

Chapter 2: The World of Pescatarian Lunch Recipes

Following are some classic pescatarian lunch recipes that are rich in healthy nutrients, and you can easily make them with the detailed instructions list in each recipe:

2.1 Buttery Grilled Shrimp Recipe

Preparation Time: 10 minutes

Cooking Time: 25 minutes

Serving: 2

Ingredients:

- Powdered cumin, one tablespoon
- Salt, to taste
- Black pepper, to taste
- Turmeric powder, one teaspoon
- Onion, one cup
- Vegetable broth, one cup
- Smoked paprika, half teaspoon
- Unboned shrimp pieces, one pound
- Minced garlic, two tablespoon
- Minced ginger, two tablespoon

- Cilantro, half cup
- Butter, two tablespoon
- Chopped tomatoes, one cup
- Grated ginger, two tablespoon

Instructions:

1. Take a pan.
2. Add the oil and onions into the pan.
3. Cook the onions until they become soft and fragrant.
4. Add in the chopped garlic and ginger.
5. Cook the mixture and add the tomatoes into it.
6. Add the spices and shrimps.
7. Mix the shrimps so that the tomatoes and spices are coated all over the shrimps.
8. Grill the shrimps for fifteen minutes.
9. When the shrimps are done, add in the cilantro.
10. The dish is ready to be served.

2.2 Fajita Styled Shrimp and Grits Recipe

Preparation Time: 30 minutes

Cooking Time: 20 minutes

Serving: 4

Ingredients:

- Shrimp pieces, three cup
- Fajita spice powder, one teaspoon
- Cooking grits, one cup
- Smoked paprika, half teaspoon
- Shredded Mexican cheese blend, half cup
- Minced garlic, two tablespoon
- Minced ginger, two tablespoon
- Orange juice, half cup
- Olive oil, two tablespoon
- Chopped tomatoes, one cup
- Bell peppers, two cups
- Salsa, one cup
- Water, four cups

Instructions:

1. Boil the water in a large saucepan.
2. Add the cooking grits into it.
3. Cook grits until the mixture turns thick.
4. Add the olive oil into a large pan.
5. Add the garlic, ginger, shrimps and fajita spice powder into the pan.
6. Cook shrimps and then add the bell peppers.
7. Add all the spices and tomatoes into the mixture.
8. Cook the mixture for five minutes and then add the orange juice into the mixture.
9. Dish out shrimp and bell peppers when they are done.
10. Add a spoon full of grits and salsa on top.
11. Your dish is ready to be served.

2.3 Pretzel Crusted Catfish Recipe

Preparation Time: 10 minutes

Cooking Time: 30 minutes

Serving: 2

Ingredients:

- Catfish, one pound
- Orange juice, one tablespoon
- Garlic powder, one tablespoon

- Chili powder, half tablespoon

- Olive oil, one cup

- Cilantro, one tablespoon

- Mayonnaise, one cup

- Avocado, two slices

- Salt to taste

- Pepper to taste

- Cooking oil, as required

- Crushed pretzels, one cup

Instructions:

1. Wash the catfish and let it dry.
2. Take a small bowl.
3. Add orange juice, garlic powder and mayonnaise into the bowl.
4. Add chili powder and pepper.
5. Then add cilantro and mix them all well.
6. Add all the ingredients together to form a smooth paste.
7. Add the catfish into the mixture and coat well.
8. Coat each catfish piece in the crusted pretzels and then deep fry the fish.
9. Dish out fish when it turns golden brown.
10. Your dish is ready to be served.

2.4 Garlic and Herb Salmon Sliders Recipe

Preparation Time: 20 minutes

Cooking Time: 20 minutes

Serving: 4

Ingredients:

- Burger buns, as required
- Minced salmon meat, one cup
- Bread crumbs, one cup
- Egg, one
- Fresh Italian herbs, half cup
- Fresh chopped cilantro, half cup
- Salt, to taste
- Black pepper, to taste
- Olive oil, for frying
- Lemon juice, a quarter cup
- Fresh chopped garlic, two tablespoon
- Butter, one tablespoon

Instructions:

1. Take a large bowl.
2. Add the salmon meat, chopped garlic, lemon juice, salt, pepper, bread crumbs and egg into it.

3. Mix all the ingredients well.

4. Add the chopped cilantro and fresh Italian herbs into the mixture.

5. Mix the ingredients until they become smooth.

6. Shape the mixture into patties.

7. In a large pan, add the olive oil and cook the patties.

8. Cook the patties until they turn golden brown from both sides.

9. Add butter on your buns and heat them.

10. Add the salmon patty on the bread slice.

11. Cover the patty with the burger bun.

12. The salmon sliders are ready to be served.

2.5 Feta and Tomato Basil Fish Recipe

Preparation Time: 10 minutes

Cooking Time: 40 minutes

Serving: 2

Ingredients:

- Fresh basil leaves, one cup
- Mix spice, one teaspoon
- Onion, one cup
- Salmon pieces, half pound
- Smoked paprika, half teaspoon

- Chopped cilantro, as required
- Minced garlic, two tablespoon
- Minced ginger, two tablespoon
- Lemon juice, half cup
- Butter, two tablespoon
- Chopped cilantro, as required
- Fresh herbs, one tablespoon
- Chopped tomatoes, one cup
- Feta cheese, one cup

Instructions:

1. Take a large pan.
2. Add in the butter and onions.
3. Cook the onions until they become soft and fragrant.
4. Add in the chopped garlic and ginger.
5. Cook the mixture and add the tomatoes into it.
6. Add the spices and feta cheese.
7. When the tomatoes are done, add the salmon pieces into it.
8. Mix the ingredients carefully and cover the pan.
9. Add in the remaining ingredients in the end and cook it for five minutes.
10. Dish out when salmon is done.
11. Garnish it with chopped fresh cilantro.
12. Your dish is ready to be served.

2.6 Grilled Pistachio and Lemon Pesto Shrimp Recipe

Preparation Time: 10 minutes

Cooking Time: 25 minutes

Serving: 2

Ingredients:

- Lemon juice, half cup
- Salt, to taste
- Black pepper, to taste
- Lemon zest, one teaspoon
- Onion, one cup
- Vegetable broth, one cup
- Smoked paprika, half teaspoon
- Unboned shrimp pieces, one pound
- Minced garlic, two tablespoon
- Minced ginger, two tablespoon
- Cilantro, half cup
- Butter, two tablespoon
- Pesto paste, one cup
- Crushed pistachio, half cup
- Grated ginger, two tablespoon

Instructions:

1. Take a large bowl.
2. Add in the chopped garlic and ginger.
3. Mix the mixture and add the pesto paste into it.
4. Add the spices and shrimps.
5. Add the rest of the ingredients into the bowl.
6. Mix the shrimps so that all the spices are coated all over the shrimps.
7. Grill the shrimps for fifteen minutes with butter.
8. Dish out the shrimps and add the cilantro on top.
9. The dish is ready to be served.

2.7 Spicy Shrimp Curry Recipe

Preparation Time: 10 minutes

Cooking Time: 40 minutes

Serving: 2

Ingredients:

- Red chili paste, two tablespoon
- Vegetable broth, one cup
- Turmeric powder, one teaspoon
- Onion, one cup
- Boneless shrimps, two cups

- Smoked paprika, half teaspoon
- Water, one cup
- Mixed vegetables, two cups
- Mix spices, two tablespoon
- Minced garlic, two tablespoon
- Minced ginger, two tablespoon
- Cilantro, half cup
- Olive oil, two tablespoon
- Chopped tomatoes, one cup

Instructions:

1. Take a pan.
2. Add the oil and onions into the pan.
3. Cook the onions until they become soft and fragrant.
4. Add in the chopped garlic and ginger.
5. Cook the mixture and add the tomatoes into it.
6. Add the spices.
7. When the tomatoes are done, add the spices into it.
8. Add in the broth, shrimps and vegetables.
9. Mix the ingredients carefully and cover your pan.
10. Cook the ingredients for fifteen to twenty minutes.
11. Add cilantro on top.
12. Your dish is ready to be served.

2.8 Chiplote and Lime Shrimp Bake Recipe

Preparation Time: 10 minutes
Cooking Time: 25 minutes
Serving: 2

Ingredients:

- Chiplote sauce, one cup
- Powdered cumin, one tablespoon
- Salt, to taste
- Black pepper, to taste
- Turmeric powder, one teaspoon
- Onion, one cup
- Lemon juice, half cup
- Vegetable broth, one cup
- Smoked paprika, half teaspoon
- Shrimp pieces, one pound
- Minced garlic, two tablespoon
- Minced ginger, two tablespoon
- Cilantro, half cup
- Olive oil, two tablespoon
- Chopped tomatoes, one cup
- Grated ginger, two tablespoon

Instructions:

1. Take a pan.
2. Add in the oil and onions.
3. Cook the onions until they become soft and fragrant.
4. Add in the chopped garlic and ginger.
5. Cook the mixture and add the tomatoes into it.
6. Add the spices, lemon juice, chiplote sauce, and shrimp.
7. Mix the shrimp so that the tomatoes and spices are coated all over the shrimp.
8. Bake the shrimp for fifteen minutes.
9. Dish out the shrimp once they are done.
10. Garnish it with chopped cilantro.
11. Your dish is ready to be served.

2.9 Lemon Shrimp with Parmesan Rice Recipe

Preparation Time: 10 minutes

Cooking Time: 25 minutes

Serving: 2

Ingredients:

- Parmesan cheese, one cup
- Powdered cumin, one tablespoon
- Salt, to taste
- Black pepper, to taste
- Turmeric powder, one teaspoon
- Onion, one cup
- Lemon juice, half cup
- Vegetable broth, one cup
- Smoked paprika, half teaspoon
- Shrimp pieces, one pound
- Minced garlic, two tablespoon
- Minced ginger, two tablespoon
- Cilantro, half cup
- Olive oil, two tablespoon
- Cooked rice, one cup
- Grated ginger, two tablespoon

Instructions:

1. Take a pan.
2. Add in the oil and onions.
3. Cook the onions until they become soft and fragrant.
4. Add in the chopped garlic and ginger.
5. Cook the mixture and add the tomatoes into it.
6. Add the spices, lemon juice and shrimps.

7. Mix the shrimps so that the tomatoes and spices are coated all over the shrimps.

8. Cook the cod for fifteen minutes.

9. Add the cooked rice and parmesan cheese into the mixture.

10.   Your dish is ready to be served.

2.10 Tuna Steak on Fettuccine Recipe

Preparation Time: 10 minutes

Cooking Time: 25 minutes

Serving: 2

Ingredients:

- Fish broth, one cup
- Turmeric powder, one teaspoon
- Onion, one cup
- Tuna pieces, one cup
- Smoked paprika, half teaspoon
- Salt and black pepper, to taste
- Minced garlic, two tablespoon
- Minced ginger, two tablespoon
- Cilantro, half cup
- Olive oil, two tablespoon
- Fettucine pasta, one pack

Instructions:

1. Take a pan.

2. Add the oil and onions into the pan.

3. Cook the onions until they become soft and fragrant.

4. Add in the chopped garlic and ginger.

5. Cook the mixture well.

6. Add the spices.

7. Add in the broth.

8. Add the tuna pieces.

9. Cook the tuna on both sides.

10. Boil fettuccine according to the instructions on the package.

11. Drain fettuccine and add it into a plate.

12. Dish out tuna pieces when the tuna pieces are done.

13. Place the tuna pieces on the fettucine.

14. Add cilantro on top.

15. Your dish is ready to be served.

2.11 Cajun Shrimp Skillet Recipe

Preparation Time: 30 minutes

Cooking Time: 20 minutes

Serving: 4

Ingredients:

- Dried thyme, half teaspoon
- Powdered ginger, half teaspoon
- Powdered garlic, half teaspoon
- Cherry tomatoes, two cups
- Cajun spice, two tablespoon
- Sea salt, to taste
- Olive oil, two tablespoon
- Onion, one
- Shrimps, one pound
- Lemon juice, one cup

Instructions:

1. Heat the olive oil in a skillet
2. Add in the powdered spices.
3. Add all the ingredients along with the shrimps.
4. Cook the mixture for five to ten minutes or until the shrimps are cooked.
5. Mix it well and cook for five additional minutes.
6. Your dish is ready to be served.

2.12 Cajun Seafood Grill Recipe

Preparation Time: 10 minutes

Cooking Time: 25 minutes

Serving: 2

Ingredients:

- Lemon juice, half cup
- Salt, to taste
- Black pepper, to taste
- Lemon zest, one teaspoon
- Onion, one cup
- Vegetable broth, one cup
- Smoked paprika, half teaspoon
- Seafood, one pound
- Minced garlic, two tablespoon
- Minced ginger, two tablespoon
- Cilantro, half cup
- Butter, two tablespoon
- Cajun seasoning, half cup
- Grated ginger, two tablespoon

Instructions:

1. Take a large bowl.
2. Add in the chopped garlic and ginger.
3. Mix the mixture and add the Cajun spice into it.
4. Add the spices and seafood.

5. Add the rest of the ingredients into the bowl.

6. Mix the seafood so that all the spices are coated all over the seafood.

7. Grill the seafood for fifteen minutes with butter.

8. Dish out the seafood shrimps and add the cilantro on top.

9. The dish is ready to be served.

2.13 Grilled Lobster Tails Recipe

Preparation Time: 10 minutes

Cooking Time: 25 minutes

Serving: 2

Ingredients:

- Lemon juice, half cup
- Salt, to taste
- Black pepper, to taste
- Lemon zest, one teaspoon
- Onion, one cup
- Vegetable broth, one cup
- Smoked paprika, half teaspoon
- Lobster tails, one pound
- Minced garlic, two tablespoon
- Minced ginger, two tablespoon

- Cilantro, half cup

- Olive oil, two tablespoon

- Tomato paste, one cup

- Grated ginger, two tablespoon

Instructions:

1. Take a large bowl.

2. Add in the chopped garlic and ginger.

3. Mix the mixture and add the tomato paste into it.

4. Add the spices and lobsters.

5. Add the rest of the ingredients into the bowl.

6. Mix the lobsters so that all the spices are coated all over the lobsters.

7. Grill the lobsters for fifteen minutes with olive oil.

8. Dish out the lobsters and add the cilantro on top.

9. The dish is ready to be served.

2.14 Scallops in Sage Cream Recipe

Preparation Time: 10 minutes

Cooking Time: 40 minutes

Serving: 2

Ingredients:

- Full cream, one cup

- Mix spice, one teaspoon

- Onion, one cup

- Scallops pieces, half pound

- Smoked paprika, half teaspoon

- Chopped cilantro, as required

- Minced garlic, two tablespoon

- Minced ginger, two tablespoon

- Lemon juice, half cup

- Butter, two tablespoon

- Chopped cilantro, as required

- Fresh herbs, one tablespoon

- Chopped tomatoes, one cup

- Chopped sage, one cup

Instructions:

1. Take a large pan.
2. Add in the butter and onions.
3. Cook the onions until they become soft and fragrant.
4. Add in the chopped garlic and ginger.
5. Cook the mixture and add the tomatoes into it.
6. Add the spices and full cream.
7. When the tomatoes are done, add the scallop pieces into it.

8. Mix the ingredients carefully and cover your pan.

9. Add in the remaining ingredients in the end and cook it for five minutes.

10.   Dish out when your scallops are done.

11.   Garnish it with chopped fresh cilantro.

12.   Your dish is ready to be served.

2.15 Shrimp Alfredo Pasta Recipe

Preparation Time: 10 minutes

Cooking Time: 25 minutes

Serving: 2

Ingredients:

- Full cream, one cup
- Italian herbs, one teaspoon
- Onion, one cup
- Shrimp pieces, one cup
- Smoked paprika, half teaspoon
- Water, one cup
- Minced garlic, two tablespoon
- Minced ginger, two tablespoon
- Cilantro, half cup
- Olive oil, two tablespoon
- Pasta, one pack

Instructions:

1. Take a pan.
2. Add the oil and onions into it.
3. Cook the onions until they become soft and fragrant.
4. Add in the chopped garlic and ginger.
5. Cook the mixture and add the shrimps into it.
6. Add the spices.
7. Add in the full cream.
8. Mix the ingredients carefully and cover your pan.
9. Boil the pasta according to the instructions on the package.
10. Drain the pasta.
11. Mix the pasta into the mixture.
12. Add cilantro on top.
13. Your dish is ready to be served.

2.16 Brown Butter Salmon with Tomatoes Recipe

Preparation Time: 10 minutes

Cooking Time: 25 minutes

Serving: 2

Ingredients:

- Powdered cumin, one tablespoon
- Salt, to taste
- Black pepper, to taste
- Turmeric powder, one teaspoon
- Onion, one cup
- Vegetable broth, one cup
- Smoked paprika, half teaspoon
- Salmon pieces, one pound
- Minced garlic, two tablespoon
- Minced ginger, two tablespoon
- Cilantro, half cup
- Butter, two tablespoon
- Cherry tomatoes, one cup
- Grated ginger, two tablespoon

Instructions:

1. Take a pan.

2. Add the oil and onions into the pan.

3. Cook the onions until they become soft and fragrant.

4. Add in the chopped garlic and ginger.

5. Cook the mixture and add the tomatoes into it.

6. Add the spices and salmon pieces.

7. Mix the salmon pieces so that the spices are coated all over the salmon pieces.

8. Cook the salmon for fifteen minutes.

9. Dish out salmon and tomatoes.

10. Garnish it with chopped cilantro.

11. The dish is ready to be served.

2.17 Salmon Avocado Salad Recipe

Preparation Time: 10 minutes

Cooking Time: 30 minutes

Serving: 2

Ingredients:

- Smoked salmon pieces, half pound
- Lemon juice, one teaspoon
- Ground ginger, a quarter teaspoon
- Avocados, two

- Chopped almonds, two tablespoon

- Pepper, as required

- Cilantro, half cup

- Salt, a quarter teaspoon

- Greek yoghurt, as required

- Salad dressing, half cup

Instructions:

1. Mix all the ingredients along with the salmon and avocados.

2. In a bowl, add the salad dressing and beat it well.

3. Drizzle the dressing on top of the salmon and avocados mixture.

4. The salad is ready to be served.

2.18 Shrimp Pasta with Lemon and Spinach Recipe

Preparation Time: 10 minutes

Cooking Time: 25 minutes

Serving: 2

Ingredients:

- Lemon juice, half cup
- Chopped spinach, two cups
- Full cream, one cup
- Italian herbs, one teaspoon
- Onion, one cup
- Shrimp pieces, one cup
- Smoked paprika, half teaspoon
- Water, one cup
- Minced garlic, two tablespoon
- Minced ginger, two tablespoon
- Cilantro, half cup
- Olive oil, two tablespoon
- Pasta, one pack

Instructions:

1. Take a pan.
2. Add the oil and onions into it.

3. Cook the onions until they become soft and fragrant.

4. Add in the chopped garlic and ginger.

5. Cook the mixture and add the shrimps into it.

6. Add the spices and lemon juice.

7. Add in the chopped spinach.

8. Mix the ingredients carefully and cover your pan.

9. Boil the pasta according to the instructions on the package.

10. Drain the pasta.

11. Mix the pasta and full cream into the mixture.

12. Add cilantro on top.

13. Your dish is ready to be served.

2.19 Pan Seared Fish Recipe

Preparation Time: 10 minutes

Cooking Time: 25 minutes

Serving: 2

Ingredients:

- Powdered cumin, one tablespoon
- Salt, to taste
- Black pepper, to taste
- Turmeric powder, one teaspoon
- Onion, one cup
- Smoked paprika, half teaspoon
- Fish filet pieces, one pound
- Minced garlic, two tablespoon
- Minced ginger, two tablespoon
- Cilantro, half cup
- Olive oil, two tablespoon

Instructions:

1. Take a large bowl.
2. Add the oil and onions into the bowl.
3. Add the chopped garlic and ginger into the bowl.
4. Add the spices.
5. Add the cilantro into it.
6. Mix all the ingredients.
7. Add the fish pieces with the mixture into a pan.
8. Cook fish pieces.
9. Dish them out when cooked properly.
10. Sprinkle some cilantro on top.
11. Your dish is ready to be served.

2.20 Grilled Harissa Shrimp with Ginger Sauce Recipe

Preparation Time: 10 minutes

Cooking Time: 25 minutes

Serving: 2

Ingredients:

- Harissa, half cup
- Salt, to taste
- Black pepper, to taste
- Lemon zest, one teaspoon
- Onion, one cup
- Vegetable broth, one cup
- Smoked paprika, half teaspoon
- Shrimp pieces, one pound
- Minced garlic, two tablespoon
- Minced ginger, two tablespoon
- Cilantro, half cup
- Olive oil, two tablespoon
- Tomato paste, one cup
- Ginger sauce, half cup

Instructions:

1. Take a large bowl.
2. Add in the chopped garlic.
3. Mix the mixture and add the tomato paste into it.
4. Add the spices and shrimps.
5. Add the rest of the ingredients into the bowl.
6. Mix the shrimps so that all the spices are coated all over the shrimps.
7. Grill the shrimps for fifteen minutes with olive oil.
8. Dish out the shrimps and add the cilantro on top.
9. The dish is ready to be served.

2.21 Salmon Skewers Recipe

Preparation Time: 10 minutes
Cooking Time: 25 minutes
Serving: 2

Ingredients:

- Lemon juice, one tablespoon
- Salt, to taste
- Black pepper, to taste
- Mix spice, one teaspoon
- Onion, one cup
- Smoked paprika, half teaspoon
- Salmon filet pieces, one pound
- Minced garlic, two tablespoon
- Minced ginger, two tablespoon
- Cilantro, half cup
- Olive oil, two tablespoon
- Wooden skewers, as required

Instructions:

1. Take a large bowl.
2. Add the oil and onions into the bowl.
3. Add the chopped garlic and ginger into the bowl.

4. Add the spices.

5. Add the cilantro into it.

6. Mix all the ingredients together.

7. Add the salmon pieces with the mixture into the wooden skewers.

8. Cook your skewers.

9. Dish them out when cooked properly.

10. Sprinkle some cilantro on top.

11. Your dish is ready to be served.

2.22 Mango Curry Shrimp Recipe

Preparation Time: 10 minutes

Cooking Time: 40 minutes

Serving: 2

Ingredients:

- Vegetable broth, one cup
- Turmeric powder, one teaspoon
- Onion, one cup
- Boneless shrimps, two cups
- Smoked paprika, half teaspoon
- Water, one cup
- Mango pieces, two cups
- Mix spices, two tablespoon
- Minced garlic, two tablespoon

- Minced ginger, two tablespoon
- Cilantro, half cup
- Olive oil, two tablespoon
- Chopped tomatoes, one cup

Instructions:

1. Take a pan.
2. Add the oil and onions into the pan.
3. Cook the onions until they become soft and fragrant.
4. Add in the chopped garlic and ginger.
5. Cook the mixture and add the tomatoes into it.
6. Add the spices.
7. When the tomatoes are done, add the spices into it.
8. Add in the broth, shrimps and mangoes.
9. Mix the ingredients carefully and cover your pan.
10. Cook the ingredients for fifteen to twenty minutes.
11. Add cilantro on top.
12. Your dish is ready to be served.

2.23 Baked Almond Crusted Cod Recipe

Preparation Time: 10 minutes

Cooking Time: 25 minutes

Serving: 2

Ingredients:

- Powdered cumin, one tablespoon
- Salt, to taste
- Black pepper, to taste
- Turmeric powder, one teaspoon
- Onion, one cup
- Smoked paprika, half teaspoon
- Dijon mustard, half cup
- Cod pieces, one pound
- Minced garlic, two tablespoon
- Minced ginger, two tablespoon
- Cilantro, half cup
- Olive oil, two tablespoon
- Almond flour, three tablespoon

- Sliced almond, half cup

Instructions:

1. Take a large bowl.
2. Add the oil and onions into the bowl.
3. Add the chopped garlic and ginger into the bowl.
4. Add the tomatoes into the bowl.
5. Add the spices.
6. Add the cilantro into it.
7. Mix all the ingredients together.
8. Add the almond flour and mix ingredients.
9. Cover codpieces with the mixture above.
10. Bake codpieces.
11. Dish them out when cooked properly.
12. Sprinkle some cilantro and sliced almond on top.
13. You can serve it with any of your preferred sauces.
14. Your dish is ready to be served.

Chapter 3: The World of Pescatarian Dinner Recipes

Following are some classic pescatarian dinner recipes that are rich in healthy nutrients and you can easily make them with the detailed instructions list in each recipe:

3.1 Stir Fried Shrimp and Mushrooms Recipe

Preparation Time: 30 minutes

Cooking Time: 10 minutes

Serving: 4

Ingredients:

- Vegetable broth, one cup
- Turmeric powder, one teaspoon
- Onion, one cup
- Mushrooms, two cups
- Smoked paprika, half teaspoon
- Water, one cup
- Shrimps, two cups
- Mixed spices, two tablespoon
- Minced garlic, two tablespoon
- Minced ginger, two tablespoon

- Cilantro, half cup
- Olive oil, two tablespoon
- Chopped tomatoes, one cup

Instructions:

1. Take a pan.
2. Add in the oil and onions.
3. Cook the onions until they become soft and fragrant.
4. Add in the chopped garlic and ginger.
5. Cook the mixture and add the tomatoes into it.
6. Add the spices and sauces.
7. When the tomatoes are done, add the shrimps and mushrooms into it.
8. Cook for five minutes.
9. When cooked, dish it out.
10. Garnish it with chopped cilantro leaves
11. Your dish is ready to be served.

3.2 Basil and Lemon Crab Linguini Recipe

Preparation Time: 10 minutes

Cooking Time: 25 minutes

Serving: 2

Ingredients:

- Lemon juice, half cup
- Chopped basil, two cups
- Full cream, one cup
- Italian herbs, one teaspoon
- Onion, one cup
- Crabmeat, one cup
- Smoked paprika, half teaspoon
- Water, one cup
- Minced garlic, two tablespoon
- Minced ginger, two tablespoon
- Cilantro, half cup
- Olive oil, two tablespoon
- Linguini, one pack

Instructions:

1. Take a pan.

2. Add the oil and onions into it.

3. Cook the onions until they become soft and fragrant.

4. Add in the chopped garlic and ginger.

5. Cook the mixture and add the crab meat into it.

6. Add the spices and lemon juice.

7. Add in the chopped basil.

8. Mix the ingredients carefully and cover your pan.

9. Boil the linguini according to the instructions on the package.

10. Drain the linguini.

11. Mix the linguini and full cream into the mixture.

12. Add cilantro on top.

13. Your dish is ready to be served.

3.3 Crab Topped Fish Fillets Recipe

Preparation Time: 25 minutes

Cooking Time: 15 minutes

Serving: 4

Ingredients:

- Chopped garlic, two teaspoon

- Green onions, three tablespoon
- Bread crumbs, half cup
- Crabmeat, two cups
- Fish filets, one pound
- Chopped fresh dill, two tablespoon
- Vegetable oil, two tablespoon
- Salt to taste
- Black pepper to taste
- Eggs, two
- Chopped onions, two tablespoon

Instructions:

1. In a large bowl, add in the onions and the garlic.
2. Add in the rest of the ingredients.
3. In a pan, heat the vegetable oil.
4. Fry the fish filets.
5. Dish out filets when they turn golden brown on both sides.
6. Your dish is ready to be served.

3.4 Pesto and Shrimp Pasta Recipe

Preparation Time: 10 minutes

Cooking Time: 25 minutes

Serving: 2

Ingredients:

- Pesto paste, half cup
- Full cream, one cup
- Italian herbs, one teaspoon
- Onion, one cup
- Shrimp pieces, one cup
- Smoked paprika, half teaspoon
- Water, one cup
- Minced garlic, two tablespoon
- Minced ginger, two tablespoon
- Cilantro, half cup
- Olive oil, two tablespoon
- Pasta, one pack

Instructions:

1. Take a pan.
2. Add the oil and onions into it.

3. Cook the onions until they become soft and fragrant.

4. Add in the chopped garlic and ginger.

5. Cook the mixture and add the shrimps into it.

6. Add the spices and pesto paste.

7. Mix the ingredients carefully and cover pan.

8. Boil the pasta according to the instructions on the package.

9. Drain the pasta.

10. Mix the pasta and full cream into the mixture.

11. Add cilantro on top.

12. Your dish is ready to be served.

3.5 Shrimp Stew Recipe

Preparation Time: 10 minutes

Cooking Time: 40 minutes

Serving: 2

Ingredients:

- Fish broth, one cup
- Turmeric powder, one teaspoon
- Onion, one cup
- Lemon juice, half cup
- Shrimp mince, half pound

- Powdered cumin, half tablespoon
- Smoked paprika, half teaspoon
- Water, one cup
- Minced garlic, two tablespoon
- Minced ginger, two tablespoon
- Cilantro, half cup
- Olive oil, two tablespoon
- Chopped tomatoes, one cup

Instructions:

1. Take a pan.
2. Add in the oil and onions.
3. Cook the onions until they become soft and fragrant.
4. Add in the chopped garlic and ginger.
5. Cook the mixture and add the tomatoes into it.
6. Add the spices and shrimp mince.
7. Add in the broth.
8. Mix the ingredients carefully and cover your pan.
9. Add cilantro on top.
10. Your dish is ready to be served.

3.6 Seared Scallops with Citrus and Herb Sauce Recipe

Preparation Time: 10 minutes

Cooking Time: 25 minutes

Serving: 2

Ingredients:

- Orange juice, one cup
- Powdered cumin, one tablespoon
- Salt, to taste
- Black pepper, to taste
- Turmeric powder, one teaspoon
- Onion, one cup
- Smoked paprika, half teaspoon
- Scallop pieces, one pound
- Minced garlic, two tablespoon
- Minced ginger, two tablespoon
- Cilantro, half cup
- Heavy cream, half cup
- Italian herbs, two tablespoon
- Olive oil, two tablespoon

Instructions:

1. Take a large bowl.

2. Add the oil and onions into the bowl.

3. Add the chopped garlic and ginger into the bowl.

4. Add the spices.

5. Add the cilantro into it.

6. Mix all the ingredients together.

7. Add the scallop pieces with the mixture into a pan.

8. Add the orange juice, herbs and heavy cream into the pan.

9. Dish them out when cooked properly.

10. Garnish with some cilantro on top.

11. Your dish is ready to be served.

3.7 Shrimp Puttanesca Recipe

Preparation Time: 10 minutes

Cooking Time: 25 minutes

Serving: 2

Ingredients:

- White wine, half cup
- Cherry tomatoes, one cup
- Italian herbs, one teaspoon
- Onion, one cup
- Green olives, half cup
- Shrimp pieces, one cup
- Smoked paprika, half teaspoon
- Water, one cup
- Minced garlic, two tablespoon
- Minced ginger, two tablespoon
- Cilantro, half cup
- Olive oil, two tablespoon
- Spaghetti, one pack

Instructions:

1. Take a pan.
2. Add the oil and onions into it.
3. Cook the onions until they become soft and fragrant.
4. Add in the chopped garlic and ginger.
5. Cook the mixture and add the shrimps into it.
6. Add the spices and cherry tomatoes.
7. Mix the ingredients carefully and cover your pan.
8. Boil the spaghetti according to the instructions on the package.
9. Drain the spaghetti.
10. Mix the spaghetti and white wine into the mixture.
11. Add green olives and cilantro on top.
12. Your dish is ready to be served.

3.8 Salmon and Spud Salad Recipe

Preparation Time: 10 minutes

Cooking Time: 30 minutes

Serving: 2

Ingredients:

- Smoked salmon pieces, half pound

- Lemon juice, one teaspoon
- Ground ginger, a quarter teaspoon
- Chopped cooked spuds, two
- Chopped almonds, two tablespoon
- Pepper, as required
- Cilantro, half cup
- Salt, a quarter teaspoon
- Greek yoghurt, as required
- Salad dressing, half cup

Instructions:

1. Mix all the ingredients along with the salmon and spuds.
2. In a bowl, add the salad dressing and beat it well.
3. Drizzle the dressing on top of the salmon and spuds mixture.
4. The salad is ready to be served.

3.9 Tomato Poached Halibut Recipe

Preparation Time: 10 minutes

Cooking Time: 30 minutes

Serving: 2

Ingredients:

- Halibut pieces, half pound
- Ground ginger, a quarter teaspoon
- Pecan pieces, two tablespoon
- Tomato paste, one cup
- Pepper, as required
- Red chili powder, one teaspoon
- Cilantro, half cup
- Salt, a quarter teaspoon
- Red chili paste, one tablespoon
- Greek yoghurt, as required
- Peanuts, half cup

Instructions:

1. Boil the halibut pieces.
2. In a large pan, add all the ingredients except the halibut pieces.
3. Cook your tomato sauce.
4. Add the halibut pieces and let them simmer for five to ten minutes.
5. Add peanuts and Greek yoghurt on top.
6. Your dish is ready to be served.

3.10 Cilantro and Lime Shrimp Recipe

Preparation Time: 10 minutes

Cooking Time: 40 minutes

Serving: 2

Ingredients:

- Onion, one cup
- Shrimp pieces, half pound
- Smoked paprika, half teaspoon
- Chopped cilantro, as required
- Minced garlic, two tablespoon
- Minced ginger, two tablespoon
- Lemon juice, half cup
- Butter, two tablespoon
- Fresh herbs, one tablespoon
- Chopped tomatoes, one cup

Instructions:

1. Take a large pan.
2. Add in the butter and onions.
3. Cook the onions until they become soft and fragrant.
4. Add in the chopped garlic and ginger.
5. Cook the mixture and add the tomatoes into it.
6. Add the salt, pepper, and fresh herbs.
7. When the tomatoes are done, add the shrimp pieces into it.

8. Mix the ingredients carefully and cover your pan.

9. When done, dish it out.

10.   Add fresh chopped cilantro on top.

11.   Your dish is ready to be served.

3.11 Citrus Scallops Recipe

Preparation Time: 10 minutes

Cooking Time: 25 minutes

Serving: 2

Ingredients:

- Orange juice, one cup
- Powdered cumin, one tablespoon
- Salt, to taste
- Black pepper, to taste
- Turmeric powder, one teaspoon
- Onion, one cup
- Smoked paprika, half teaspoon
- Scallop pieces, one pound
- Minced garlic, two tablespoon
- Minced ginger, two tablespoon
- Cilantro, half cup
- Lemon juice, half cup
- Olive oil, two tablespoon

Instructions:

1. Take a large bowl.

2. Add the oil and onions into the bowl.

3. Add the chopped garlic and ginger into the bowl.

4. Add the spices.

5. Add the cilantro into it.

6. Mix all the ingredients together.

7. Add the scallop pieces with the mixture into a pan.

8. Add the orange juice, and lemon juice into the pan.

9. Dish them out when cooked properly.

10.   Garnish with some cilantro on top.

11.   Your dish is ready to be served.

3.12 Rosemary and Garlic Shrimp Recipe

Preparation Time: 30 minutes

Cooking Time: 10 minutes

Serving: 4

Ingredients:

- Vegetable broth, one cup

- Turmeric powder, one teaspoon

- Onion, one cup

- Rosemary herbs, half cup
- Smoked paprika, half teaspoon
- Water, one cup
- Shrimps, two cups
- Mixed spices, two tablespoon
- Minced garlic, two tablespoon
- Cilantro, half cup
- Olive oil, two tablespoon
- Chopped tomatoes, one cup

Instructions:

1. Take a pan.
2. Add in the oil and onions.
3. Cook the onions until they become soft and fragrant.
4. Add in the chopped garlic.
5. Cook the mixture and add the tomatoes into it.
6. Add the spices and sauces.
7. When the tomatoes are done, add the shrimps and rosemary herbs into it.
8. Cook for five minutes.
9. When cooked, dish it out.
10. Garnish it with chopped cilantro leaves
11. Your dish is ready to be served.

3.13 Spicy Mango Scallops Recipe

Preparation Time: 10 minutes

Cooking Time: 40 minutes

Serving: 2

Ingredients:

- Red chili paste, two tablespoon
- Turmeric powder, one teaspoon
- Onion, one cup
- Scallops, two cups
- Smoked paprika, half teaspoon
- Water, one cup
- Mango pieces, two cups
- Mix spices, two tablespoon
- Minced garlic, two tablespoon
- Minced ginger, two tablespoon
- Cilantro, half cup
- Olive oil, two tablespoon
- Chopped tomatoes, one cup

Instructions:

1. Take a pan.
2. Add the oil and onions into the pan.

3. Cook the onions until they become soft and fragrant.

4. Add in the chopped garlic and ginger.

5. Cook the mixture and add the tomatoes into it.

6. Add the spices.

7. When the tomatoes are done, add the spices into it.

8. Add in the red chili paste, scallops and mangoes.

9. Mix the ingredients carefully and cover your pan.

10. Cook the ingredients for fifteen to twenty minutes.

11. Add cilantro on top.

12. Your dish is ready to be served.

3.14 Cornmeal Catfish with Avocado Sauce Recipe

Preparation Time: 10 minutes

Cooking Time: 30 minutes

Serving: 2

Ingredients:

- Catfish, one pound
- Orange juice, one tablespoon
- Garlic powder, one teaspoon
- Lemon juice, half cup

- Chili powder, half tablespoon
- Olive oil, one cup
- Cilantro, one tablespoon
- Salt to taste
- Pepper to taste
- Cooking oil, as required
- Crushed cornmeal, one cup
- Avocado sauce, as required

Instructions:

1. Wash the catfish and let it dry.
2. Take a small bowl.
3. Add orange juice, garlic powder and lemon juice into the bowl.
4. Add chili powder and pepper.
5. Then add cilantro and mix them all well.
6. Add all the ingredients together to form a smooth paste.
7. Add the catfish into the mixture and coat well.
8. Coat each catfish piece in the crusted cornmeal, and then deep fry the fish.
9. Dish out your fish when it turns golden brown.
10. Drizzle the avocado sauce on top of the catfish.
11. Your dish is ready to be served.

3.15 Lime Boiled Catfish Recipe

Preparation Time: 10 minutes
Cooking Time: 30 minutes
Serving: 2

Ingredients:

- Catfish, one pound
- Orange juice, one tablespoon
- Garlic powder, one teaspoon
- Chili powder, half tablespoon
- Olive oil, one cup
- Cilantro, one tablespoon
- Salt to taste
- Pepper to taste
- Cooking oil, as required
- Lime juice, one cup
- Lime zest, one tablespoon

Instructions:

1. Wash the catfish and let it dry.
2. Take a small bowl.

3. Add orange juice, garlic powder, lime zest and lime juice into the bowl.

4. Add chili powder and pepper.

5. Then add cilantro and mix them all well.

6. Add all the ingredients together to form a smooth paste.

7. Add the catfish into the mixture and coat well.

8. Steam the fish.

9. Dish out the fish when it cooks properly.

10.   You can serve it with any sauce.

11.   Your dish is ready to be served.

3.16 Southwestern Catfish Recipe

Preparation Time: 10 minutes

Cooking Time: 25 minutes

Serving: 2

Ingredients:

- Mix spice, one tablespoon
- Salt, to taste
- Black pepper, to taste
- Turmeric powder, one teaspoon
- Onion, one cup
- Smoked paprika, half teaspoon
- Catfish pieces, one pound

- Minced garlic, two tablespoon
- Minced ginger, two tablespoon
- Cilantro, half cup
- Olive oil, two tablespoon
- Chopped tomatoes, one cup
- Grated ginger, two tablespoon

Instructions:

1. Take a pan.
2. Add the oil and onions into the pan.
3. Cook the onions until they become soft and fragrant.
4. Add in the chopped garlic and ginger.
5. Cook the mixture and add the tomatoes into it.
6. Add the spices and catfish.
7. Mix the catfish so that the tomatoes and spices are coated all over the catfish.
8. Grill the shrimps for fifteen minutes.
9. Garnish with chopped cilantro.
10. The dish is ready to be served.

3.17 Breaded Sea Scallops Recipe

Preparation Time: 10 minutes

Cooking Time: 30 minutes

Serving: 2

Ingredients:

- Garlic powder, one cup
- Chili powder, half tablespoon
- Olive oil, one cup
- Scallops, one pound
- Cilantro, one tablespoon
- Mayonnaise, one cup
- Bread crumbs, two cups
- Salt to taste
- Pepper to taste

Instructions:

1. Wash the scallops and let it dry.
2. Take a small bowl.
3. Add the scallops into it.
4. Add all the spices.
5. Add salt and pepper as required.
6. Then add cilantro and mix them all well.
7. Marinate the scallops for an hour.
8. After marinating, coat the fish in the bread crumbs.

9. Fry it until the scallops turn golden brown.

10.   Your dish is ready to be served.

3.18 Deep Fried Catfish Recipe

Preparation Time: 10 minutes

Cooking Time: 30 minutes

Serving: 2

Ingredients:

- Catfish, one pound
- Orange juice, one tablespoon
- Garlic powder, one teaspoon
- Lemon juice, half cup
- Chili powder, half tablespoon
- Olive oil, one cup
- Cilantro, one tablespoon
- Chopped parsley, as required
- Salt to taste
- Pepper to taste
- Cooking oil, as required

Instructions:

1. Wash the catfish and let it dry.

2. Take a small bowl.

3. Add orange juice, garlic powder and lemon juice into the bowl.

4. Add chili powder and pepper.

5. Then add cilantro and mix them all well.

6. Add all the ingredients together to form a smooth paste.

7. Add the catfish into the mixture and coat well.

8. Deep fry the catfish.

9. Dish out your fish when it turns golden brown.

10. Add fresh chopped parsley on top.

11. Your dish is ready to be served.

3.19 One Pot Roasted Halibut Recipe

Preparation Time: 10 minutes

Cooking Time: 30 minutes

Serving: 2

Ingredients:

- Turmeric powder, one teaspoon
- Onion, one cup
- Halibut filet pieces, half pound
- Smoked paprika, half teaspoon
- Minced garlic, two tablespoon
- Minced ginger, two tablespoon
- Lemon juice, half cup
- Olive oil, two tablespoon
- Chopped tomatoes, one cup

Instructions:

1. Take a pan.
2. Add in the oil and onions.
3. Cook the onions until they become soft and fragrant.
4. Add in the chopped garlic and ginger.
5. Cook the mixture and add the tomatoes into it.
6. Add the spices.
7. When the tomatoes are done, add the halibut pieces into it.
8. Mix the ingredients carefully and place your mixture into the oven.
9. Add cilantro on top.

10.   Drizzle any preferred sauce on top of your fish.

11.   Your dish is ready to be served.

3.20 Instant Pot Steamed Cod with Ginger Sauce Recipe

Preparation time: 10 minutes

Cooking Time: 20 minutes

Serving: 4

Ingredients:

- Cod, one pound
- Ginger sauce, half cup
- Lime juice, half cup
- Lemon juice, half cup
- Tomatoes, two
- Red onion, one cup
- Cilantro, half cup
- Salt, to taste
- Pepper, to taste

Instructions:

1. Heat an instant pot.
2. Add all the ingredients into the pot.
3. Add the cod pieces into the mixture.
4. Cover the instant pot.
5. Dish out the mixture when the cod is cooked.

6. Garnish it with chopped cilantro on top.

7. Your dish is ready to be served.

3.21 Shrimp Stuffed Avocados Recipe

Preparation time: 10 minutes

Cooking Time: 20 minutes

Serving: 4

Ingredients:

- Shrimp, one pound
- Avocados, as required
- Lime juice, half cup
- Lemon juice, half cup
- Tomatoes, two
- Red onion, one cup
- Cilantro, half cup
- Cucumber, half cup
- Salt, to taste
- Pepper, to taste

Instructions:

1. Bring a pot of water to boil.

2. Add the shrimp to boiling water and cook it in steam.

3. Drain the shrimp and add it in the ice water.

4. Take a large bowl and add the shrimp into it.

5. Add the lemon juice, lime juice and cilantro into it.

6. Add the pepper and salt in it to season it.

7. Mix them thoroughly.

8. Peel the avocados and remove the seed.

9. Add the mixture into the avocados and serve.

10. Your dish is ready to be served.

3.22 Cod and Pesto Pasta Recipe

Preparation time: 30 minutes

Cooking Time: 40 minutes

Serving: 4

Ingredients:

- Pesto pasta, one cup
- Cod, one pound
- Minced garlic, two tablespoon
- Minced ginger, two tablespoon
- Cilantro, half cup
- Sesame oil, two tablespoon
- Corn flour, two tablespoon

- Water, half cup
- Vegetable stock, two cup
- Chopped tomatoes, one cup
- Italian parsley, one cup
- Onion, one cup
- Pasta, one pack
- Oregano, one teaspoon
- Water, one cup

Instructions:

1. Take a pan.
2. Add in the oil and onions.
3. Cook the onions until they become soft and fragrant.
4. Add the cod and pesto into it.
5. Add in the chopped garlic and ginger.
6. Cook the mixture and add the tomatoes into it.
7. Add the spices, sauces and white wine.
8. When the tomatoes are done, add the pasta into it.
9. Add in the vegetable broth.
10. Mix the ingredients carefully and cover your pan.
11. Cook the mixture for twenty minutes.
12. Add cilantro on top.
13. Your dish is ready to be served.

3.23 Steamed Shrimps with Mint Recipe

Preparation Time: 10 minutes

Cooking Time: 20 minutes

Serving: 4

Ingredients:

- Shrimp, one pound
- Mint sauce, half cup
- Lime juice, half cup
- Lemon juice, half cup
- Tomatoes, two
- Red onion, one cup
- Cilantro, half cup
- Salt, to taste
- Pepper, to taste

Instructions:

1. Bring a pot of water to boil.
2. Add the shrimp to boiling water and cook it in steam.
3. Drain the shrimp and add it in the ice water.
4. Take a large bowl and add the shrimp into it.
5. Add the lemon juice, lime juice and cilantro into it.

6. Add the pepper and salt in it to season it.

7. Mix them thoroughly.

8. Steam it for ten minutes.

9. Add the mint sauce as required.

10.   Your dish is ready to be served.

Chapter 4: The World of Pescatarian Snack Recipes

Following are some yummy pescatarian snack recipes that are rich in healthy nutrients, and you can easily make them with the detailed instructions list in each recipe:

4.1 Avocado Crab Boats Recipe

Preparation time: 10 minutes

Cooking Time: 25 minutes

Serving: 4

Ingredients:

- Avocados, two
- Eggs, two
- Salt, one tablespoon
- Pepper, to taste
- Bread crumbs, one cup
- Vegetable oil, one cup
- Flour, half cup
- Water, half cup

Instructions:

1. Take a saucepan and heat it well.
2. Add the vegetable oil into it.
3. Heat the oil and cut the avocado in slices.
4. Take a bowl and add the flour into it.
5. Add the eggs, salt and pepper.
6. Mix them gently and add the avocado slices into it.
7. Then coat the avocado slices into the bread crumbs.
8. Fry it well until it becomes brown.
9. Your dish is ready to be served.

4.2 Fish and Fries Recipe

Preparation time: 10 minutes

Cooking Time: 25 minutes

Serving: 4

Ingredients:

- Flour, half cup
- Fish, one pound
- Potato, one cup
- Ginger, one tablespoon
- Garlic powder, two teaspoon
- Salt, to taste

Instructions:

1. Take a saucepan and heat it well.
2. Add the vegetable oil into it.
3. Heat the oil and cut the fish in pieces.
4. Take a bowl and add the flour into it.
5. Add the garlic powder and ginger in it.
6. Then add the eggs, salt and pepper.
7. Mix them gently and make a paste-type mixture.
8. Add the fish pieces into it.
9. Coat the fish pieces into bread crumbs.
10. Fry it until it becomes brown.
11. Your dish is ready to be served.

4.3 Classic Crab Cakes Recipe

Preparation time: 30 minutes

Cooking Time: 25 minutes

Serving: 4

Ingredients:

- All-purpose flour, one cup
- Crabmeat, one cup
- Baking powder, one tablespoon

- Baking soda, half tablespoon
- Egg, two
- Milk, one cup
- Vegetable oil, one cup
- Salt, half tablespoon
- Oil, one cup

Instructions:

1. Take a large bowl and add the all-purpose flour in it
2. Add the crab meat in it and mix well.
3. Add the baking powder, and salt into it.
4. Mix well until a good mixture is obtained.
5. Take another bowl and add the eggs into it.
6. Add the milk and a little oil into it.
7. Combine them well, so that a good mixture is formed.
8. Form round balls from the crab mixture and then dip it into the egg mixture.
9. Fry the balls until a light brown color comes.
10. Your dish is ready to be served.

4.4 Skinny Crab Quiche Recipe

Preparation time: 20 minutes

Cooking Time: 20 minutes

Serving: 4

Ingredients:

- Crabmeat, one cup
- Pie crust, two
- Heavy cream, one cup
- Cheese, one cup
- Green onions, one cup
- Baking soda, half tablespoon
- Egg, two
- Milk, one cup
- Vegetable oil, one cup
- Salt, half tablespoon
- Oil, one cup

Instructions:

1. Take a large bowl and add the all-purpose flour in it
2. Add the crab meat in it and mix well.
3. Add the baking powder, and salt into it.
4. Mix well until a good mixture is obtained.
5. Take another bowl and add the eggs into it.
6. Add the milk into it and a little oil into it.
7. Combine the mixture in both bowls.
8. Bake the pie crust for ten minutes.

9. Pour the above-prepared mixture into it.

10.   Bake it for twenty minutes until a light brown color comes.

11.   Your dish is ready to be served.

4.5 Asian Salmon Tacos Recipe

Preparation time: 20 minutes

Cooking Time: 20 minutes

Serving: 2

Ingredients:

- Salmon, one pound
- Green onion, half cup
- Kosher salt, one tablespoon
- Tomatoes, two
- Avocado slices, two
- Cilantro, to garnish
- Red onions, one cup
- Ginger, one tablespoon
- Garlic powder, two teaspoon
- Sesame oil, one teaspoon
- Salt, to taste
- Pepper, to taste

Instructions:

1. Take a large bowl and add salmon pieces into it.

2. Add the ginger and garlic powder to it.

3. Add the tomatoes and red onion into it.

4. Mix well until a good mixture is obtained.

5. Add the soy sauce and mix well.

6. Toss the cilantro into the sauce.

7. Add the salt and pepper as you like.

8. Cook the salmon mixture for twenty minutes.

9. Bake it until it becomes golden and slightly crisp.

10. Once the salmon is cooked, fill the tacos with it.

11. Your dish is ready to be served.

4.6 Seafood Ceviche Recipe

Preparation time: 10 minutes

Cooking Time: 20 minutes

Serving: 4

Ingredients:

- Shrimp, one pound
- Lime juice, half cup
- Lemon juice, half cup
- Tomatoes, two
- Red onion, one cup
- Cilantro, half cup

- Cucumber, half cup

- Avocado slices, one cup

- Salt, to taste

- Pepper, to taste

Instructions:

8. Bring a pot of water to boil.

9. Add the shrimp to boiling water and cook it.

10. Drain the shrimp and add it in the ice water.

11. Take a large bowl and add the shrimp into it.

12. Add the lemon juice, lime juice and cilantro into it.

13. Add the pepper and salt in it to season it.

14. Mix them thoroughly.

15. Refrigerate it for thirty minutes.

16. Add the cucumber and avocado slices on top.

17. Your dish is ready to be served.

4.7 Salmon Sticks with Hummus Recipe

Preparation time: 30 minutes

Cooking Time: 25 minutes

Serving: 4

Ingredients:

- Hummus, one cup
- Salmon fillets, four
- Arugula, two cups
- Cilantro, one
- Red bell pepper, one tablespoon
- Cheese, one cup
- Whole wheat panko, one cup
- Butter, half cup
- Honey, two tablespoon
- Lemon juice, one cup
- Garlic powder, two tablespoon
- Ginger, one tablespoon
- Soy sauce, one tablespoon
- Salt, to taste
- Sriracha, as required

Instructions:

1. Take a large bowl and add the salmon fillets into it.
2. Add the ginger and garlic powder to it.
3. Mix well until a good mixture is obtained.
4. Add the cilantro and mix gently.
5. Add the panko, cheese and honey into it.

6. Distribute the mixture evenly over the salmon fillets.

7. Add the lemon juice, olive oil and soy sauce.

8. Add the salt and pepper as you like.

9. Bake the salmon for twenty minutes

10. Serve the sticks with hummus.

11. Your dish is ready to be served.

4.8 Tuna Fritters Recipe

Preparation time: 20 minutes

Cooking Time: 10 minutes

Serving: 4

Ingredients:

- Cheese, one cup
- Tuna, three
- Bread crumbs, three
- Diced onion, one cup
- Vegetable oil, one cup
- Salt, one tablespoon
- Milk, one cup
- Black pepper, one tablespoon
- Eggs, two
- Lemon juice, one tablespoon

Instructions:

1. Take a saucepan and heat it well.
2. Add the vegetable oil into it.
3. Heat the oil and cut the fish in pieces.
4. Take a bowl and add the flour into it.
5. Add the garlic powder and ginger in it.
6. Then add the eggs, salt and pepper.
7. Add the cheese and diced onions into it.
8. Mix them gently and make a paste-type material.
9. Then add the tuna pieces into it.
10. Then coat the tuna pieces into bread crumbs.
11. Fry it well until it becomes light brown.
12. Your dish is ready to be served.

4.9 Roasted Salmon Fries Recipe

Preparation time: 15 minutes

Cooking Time: 25 minutes

Serving: 4

Ingredients:

- Flour, half cup
- Salmon Fish, one pound
- Potato, one cup
- Ginger, one tablespoon
- Garlic powder, two teaspoon
- Salt, to taste
- Pepper, to taste
- Bread crumbs, as required

Instructions:

1. Take a saucepan and heat it well.
2. Add the vegetable oil into it.
3. Heat the oil and cut the fish in pieces.
4. Take a bowl and add the flour into it.
5. Add the garlic powder and Ginger in it.
6. Then add the eggs, salt and pepper.

7. Mix them gently and make a paste-type material.

8. Then add the fish pieces into it.

9. Then coat the fish pieces into bread crumbs.

10.   Fry it well until it becomes brown.

11.   Your dish is ready to be served.

4.10 Fish Stuffed Mushrooms Recipe

. **Preparation time:** 20 minutes

Cooking Time: 20 minutes

Serving: 2

Ingredients:

- Fish, one pound
- Mushrooms, one pound
- Bread crumbs, as required
- Green onion, half cup
- Kosher salt, one tablespoon
- Tomatoes, two
- Avocado slices, two
- Cilantro, to garnish
- Red onions, one cup
- Ginger, one tablespoon
- Garlic powder, two teaspoon
- Sesame oil, one teaspoon
- Salt, to taste

Instructions:

1. Take a large bowl and add fish pieces into it.
2. Add the ginger and garlic powder to it.
3. Add the tomatoes and red onion into it.
4. Mix well until a good mixture is obtained.
5. Add the soy sauce and mix well.
6. Toss the cilantro into the sauce.
7. Add the salt and pepper as you like.
8. Cook the fish mixture for twenty minutes.
9. Once the fish is cooked, fill the mushrooms with it.
10. Bake it until it becomes golden and slightly crisp.
11. Your dish is ready to be served.

4.11 Fish Pie Fillets Recipe

Preparation time: 30 minutes

Cooking Time: 25 minutes

Serving: 4

Ingredients:

• Fish fillets, four

• Arugula, two cups

- Cilantro, one
- Red bell pepper, one tablespoon
- Cheese, one cup
- Whole wheat panko, one cup
- Butter, half cup
- Honey, two tablespoon
- Lemon juice, one cup
- Garlic powder, two tablespoon
- Ginger, one tablespoon
- Soy sauce, one tablespoon
- Salt, to taste
- Sriracha, as required

Instructions:

1. Take a large bowl and add the Fish fillets into it.
2. Add the ginger and garlic powder to it.
3. Mix well until a good mixture is obtained.
4. Add the cilantro and mix gently.
5. Add the panko, cheese and honey into it.
6. Distribute the mixture evenly over the fish fillets.
7. Add the lemon juice, olive oil and soy sauce.
8. Add the salt and pepper as you like.
9. Bake the fish for twenty minutes
10. Your dish is ready to be served.

4.12 Fish Pasta Soup Recipe

Preparation time: 30 minutes

Cooking Time: 40 minutes

Serving: 4

Ingredients:

- Pasta, two cups
- Eggs, two
- Fish, one pound
- Minced garlic, two tablespoon
- Minced ginger, two tablespoon
- Cilantro, half cup
- Sesame oil, two tablespoon
- Corn flour, two tablespoon
- Water, half cup
- Vegetable stock, two cup
- Chopped tomatoes, one cup
- Italian parsley, one cup
- Onion, one cup
- Mixed vegetables, half pound
- Oregano, one teaspoon
- Water, one cup

Instructions:

1. Take a pan.
2. Add in the oil and onions.
3. Cook the onions until they become soft and fragrant.
4. Add in the chopped garlic and ginger.
5. Cook the mixture and add the tomatoes into it.
6. Add the spices and sauces and the white wine.
7. When the tomatoes are done, add the mixed vegetables into it.
8. Add the vegetable broth and pasta into the pan.
9. Mix the ingredients carefully and cover your pan.
10. Boil the mixture for twenty minutes.
11. Mix the soup continuously for five minutes.
12. Add cilantro on top.
13. Your dish is ready to be served.

Conclusion

In the current world, we have become exceptionally aware of our wellbeing. We generally favor a natural eating regimen over other falsely developed food sources. Being on a tight eating routine has been the most well-known answer we get when we get some information about someone's wellbeing. It is a renowned saying, "your wellbeing is straightforwardly relative to your emotional health," on the off chance that you practice good eating habits and eat right, you are continually going to have inspiring and positive thinking towards life.

This cookbook incorporates 70 healthy plans that contain pescatarian breakfast, pescatarian lunch, pescatarian dinner, and pescatarian snack recipes that you can undoubtedly make at home without the help of any kind. Start cooking with this amazing and easy cookbook.

www.ingramcontent.com/pod-product-compliance
Lightning Source LLC
Chambersburg PA
CBHW052052150726
48002CB00002B/860